YOUR KNOWLEDGE HAS VALUE

- We will publish your bachelor's and master's thesis, essays and papers

- Your own eBook and book - sold worldwide in all relevant shops

- Earn money with each sale

Upload your text at www.GRIN.com
and publish for free

Bibliographic information published by the German National Library:

The German National Library lists this publication in the National Bibliography; detailed bibliographic data are available on the Internet at http://dnb.dnb.de .

This book is copyright material and must not be copied, reproduced, transferred, distributed, leased, licensed or publicly performed or used in any way except as specifically permitted in writing by the publishers, as allowed under the terms and conditions under which it was purchased or as strictly permitted by applicable copyright law. Any unauthorized distribution or use of this text may be a direct infringement of the author s and publisher s rights and those responsible may be liable in law accordingly.

Imprint:

Copyright © 2014 GRIN Verlag
Print and binding: Books on Demand GmbH, Norderstedt Germany
ISBN: 9783668658387

This book at GRIN:

https://www.grin.com/document/416096

Peter Krause

The Sharia. Where did Islamic Law come from?

GRIN Verlag

GRIN - Your knowledge has value

Since its foundation in 1998, GRIN has specialized in publishing academic texts by students, college teachers and other academics as e-book and printed book. The website www.grin.com is an ideal platform for presenting term papers, final papers, scientific essays, dissertations and specialist books.

Visit us on the internet:

http://www.grin.com/

http://www.facebook.com/grincom

http://www.twitter.com/grin_com

Where did Islamic Law come from?

Essay

Islamic Law and Society
ARA 2132

Lecturers:

15 November 2014 – Exeter

Thinking about where Islamic Law comes from, we have to distinguish between the scientific side, *fiqh*, and the religious side, the revealed texts.[1] With God as the legislator, society has to incorporate the given rules into daily life. However they are not always clear, so frictions are attempted to be solved using the four sources of Islamic Law.[2] Hence, Islamic Law can not exist just as a fixed statute, which regulates rights and duties of Muslims.[3] It is more a method to interpret what the law includes, influenced strongly by the opinions of different legal scholars. There exists therefore an uncertainty in what the law finally includes, because of disagreements between scholars, called *ikhtilāf*.[4]

'*Sharī'ah*' is often mentioned in connection with Islamic Law. The original meaning is God's will, but now is used as a term for the Islamic legal rules applied to the lives of Muslims.[5] The applicable rules are the achievements of scholars, who tried to interpret God's will. God's will is expressed in the primary Islamic texts, the *Qur'an* and the *Sunnah*. This is the Revelation.[6] The *Qur'an* is the word of God, written down in text form.[7] It contains rules, which are free of uncertainty.[8] On one side, the *Qur'an* is general in many cases and arising problems can only be solved by the help of the *Sunnah*. Conversely, the *Qur'an* can be specific in telling stories about very detailed cases. Conversely, the *Qur'an* can be specific in telling stories about very detailed cases. Then it is

---

1 N Calder and others, 'Law' [1] in *OEIW. Oxford Islamic Studies Online*, <http://http://www.oxfordislamicstudies.com/article/opr/t236/e0473> ac It contains rules, which are free of uncertainty in their content cessed 5th November 2014
2 K Vikor, *'Between God and the Sultan: A History of Islamic Law'* (2005), Preface v
3 K Vikor, *loc. cit.*, p.1
4 K Vikor, *loc. cit.*, p.1
5 K Vikor, *loc. cit.*, p.2
6 N Calder, *loc. cit.*, [2]
7 K A El Fadl, *'Speaking in God's Name: Islamic Law, Authority, and Women'* (2001), p.100
8 K Vikor, *loc. cit.*, p.32

possible to create a general rule from a specific case.[9]

Beside the *Qur'an*, exists the *Sunnah* as another source of Islamic Law, equal to the *Qur'an*.[10] The *Sunnah* represents the actions and sayings of the Prophet Mohammed himself.[11] They are written down in text form as well, called *hadīth*.[12] A *hadīth* is divisible in two parts. These two parts are the *isnād* and the *matn*. *Isnād* mentions the names of the direct source and the transmitters.[13] After the *isnād* follows the *matn*. It contains the action or saying of the Prophet. Sometimes the matn can be about actions or sayings of students or companions of Mohammed.[14] In contrast to the *Qur'an*, *ahadīth* are not free of uncertainty.[15] This is due to the number of *ahadīth* and the method of oral transmission through the *isnād*.[16] This increases the possibility of loosing important details of the *hadīth* or to add falsities. From this it follows that a *hadīth* has to be proven. Firstly, the *isnād* is disputable, it must be clarified if the narrators between the action or saying and the final written formulation are trustworthy. Secondly, the text of the *hadīth* can be interpreted in different ways. Thus, it must be ensured that a suitable person interprets it.[17] Thirdly, there are contradictory *ahadīth* about the same topic or the same action. Resulting from that, it is possible to categorise *hadīth* in *sahīh*[18] and *da'if*,[19,20] practised by legal scholars.[21] The *Qur'an* and the *Sunnah*, summarised under the headline

---
9 K Vikor, *loc. cit.*, p.36
10 K A El Fadl, *loc. cit.*, p.100
11 K A El Fadl, *loc. cit.*, p.100
12 Arabic plural: ahadīth
13 Isnād = chain of narrators, which transmitted the story orally
14 K Vikor, *loc. cit.*, p.38-9
15 K Vikor, *loc. cit.*, p.32
16 K A El Fadl, *loc. cit.*, p.101
17 K A El Fadl, *loc. cit.*, p.101
18 = trustworthy
19 = less trustworthy
20 K Vikor, *loc. cit.*, p. 41
21 K Vikor, *loc. cit.*, p. 41

'Revelation', can be qualified as the first "level in the process of establishing the law".[22]

Therefore, the requirement to test the *ahadīth* were the initial point of the examination with the juristic understanding process.[23] A main point of this process is to conceive what God wants by studying the revealed texts, this science is called *fiqh*.[24] In the middle of the eighth-century,[25] some legal scholars acquired a diversified knowledge of the actions and sayings of the Prophet by working intensely on *fiqh*.[26] They also interpreted the *ahadīth*, but every one in a different way. Some scholars interpreted quite strictly and literally close to the written texts, denying that there is a law beyond the *Qur'an*, the *Sunnah* and the traditions, others took a more flexible approach.[27] By and by, four big opinion leaders became increasingly important. Their names were Abū Hanīfa, Mālik b. Anas, Muhammad b. Idrīs al-Shāfi'ī and Ahmad b. Hanbal.[28] Later, the four Sunnī schools of law: the Hanafi school, the Maliki school, the Shafi'i school and the Hanbali school, were founded, named after the big legal scholars. The Arabic term for the schools is '*madhhabs*'.[29] They consolidated *fiqh* as 'study of law'.[30] These lawyers, especially Shāfi'ī, developed a methodology to compose actual legal rules considering the texts of the *Qur'an* and the *Sunnah*.[31] The process starting from rare religious texts to a legal rule is called *ijtihād*.[32] The *madhhabs* specified this for their own school by using

---
22 K Vikor, *loc. cit.*, p.31
23 N Calder, *loc. cit.*, [2]
24 K Vikor, *loc. cit.*, p.27
25 N Calder, *loc. cit.*, [2]
26 K Vikor, *loc. cit.*, p.22
27 K Vikor, *loc. cit.*, p.23
28 N J Coulson, *A History of Islamic Law* (1964), p.86 et seq.
29 N J Coulson, *loc. cit.*, p.86
30 K Vikor, *loc. cit.*, p.28
31 K Vikor, *loc. cit.*, p.31
32 K Vikor, *loc. cit.*, p.31

particular methods. But all in all, there are two important instruments, which represent the second and third level of establishing Islamic Law.[33] These are *ijmā'* and *qiyās*.

Ijmā' is the third source of Islamic Law, after the *Qur'an* and the *Sunnah*. The literal meaning of '*ijmā'*' is 'what our society [where we live] agrees on'.[34] It describes the consensus between all Muslims.[35] The idea behind this source is that Muslim society could not agree on a topic and form a view, which is in conflict with the Revelation.[36] There cannot be consensus in the community, which at the same time disagrees with the *Qur'an* and the *Sunnah*. Consequently, *ijmā'* is the result of *ijtihād*.[37] By ascertaining God's will through consensus in society, they establish a legal rule. In practise, consensus only exists about very general and undoubted topics.[38] Regarding the categories of *Ahkam*, such topics are often under Islamic commandments of *fard* or *wājib*[39] and *haram*[40]. An undoubted topic in the category of *wājib*, which Muslim society reached a consensus on is the performance of the daily prayer.[41] There are juristic disagreements in connection to the third source of Islamic Law. It is debatable who has to reach the consensus – legal scholars or the whole society. The convincing majority established the idea that consensus between the scholars is crucial.[42] Furthermore, it must be clarified which scholars are adequate to form an opinion on a topic.[43] This is a question of qualification and

---

33 K Vikor, *loc. cit.*, p.31
34 K Vikor, *loc. cit.*, p.78
35 K Vikor, *loc. cit.*, p.352
36 N J Coulson, *loc. cit.*, p.59
37 N J Coulson, *loc. cit.*, p.78
38 N J Coulson, *loc. cit.*, p.59
39 = Cumpolsory actions
40 = Sinful actions
41 N J Coulson, *loc. cit.*, p.59
42 K Vikor, *loc. cit.*, p.79
43 K A El Fadl, *loc. cit.*, p.64

degree of legal scholars. In this case, majority view is that every legal scholar should count for reaching the consensus. In this case, majority view is that every legal scholar should count for reaching the consensus, irrespective of whether he is a *mubtadi*[44,45] or not.[46] Moreover, there is the question if reached consensus, limited to regional areas, is enough or if the consensus should be extended on all legal scholars of global Muslim society.[47] The prevailing view on this problem is that all legal scholars should reach consensus on the problematic question,[48] and if one single view of a scholar varies from majority, reaching consensus becomes impossible.[49] Clarification is also needed in the question about expression of agreement or disagreement.[50] Considering that every legal Muslim scholar worldwide should agree, it is logical that it should be sufficient to express the agreement silently. This is also the standard opinion on this issue.[51] Additionally, it is important to think about the problem, if there is a chance for later *ijmā'*, when there existed a disagreement in earlier generations.[52] The majority says that a disagreement in earlier generations of scholars can not be rejected and changed to an *ijmā'* by later legal scholars.[53] Considering these aspects, *ijmā'* can be achieved on basis of the Revelation. It must be at least an 'indubitable indication' in the *Qur'an* or the *Sunnah*.[54] These strict approaches, focusing on including as many opinions of legal scholars, show effort to achieve unity in Islamic Law through the third source *ijmā'*.[55]

---

44 = someone, who acts varied from the established doctrine
45 K Vikor, *loc. cit.*, p.356
46 K Vikor, *loc. cit.*, p.79
47 K A El Fadl, *loc. cit.*, p.64
48 K Vikor, *loc. cit.*, p.80
49 K Vikor, *loc. cit.*, p.81
50 K A El Fadl, *loc. cit.*, p.64
51 K Vikor, *loc. cit.*, p.82
52 K A El Fadl, *loc. cit.*, p.64
53 K Vikor, *loc. cit.*, p.84-5
54 K Vikor, *loc. cit.*, p.85
55 N J Coulson, *loc. cit.*, p.59

Consensus about a topic leads to an agreement about the clarification of God's will and establishes a legal rule as a result.[56]

The requirement for *ijmā'* is the single opinion of a legal scholar, formed by work with the *Qur'an* and the *Sunnah*, such as interpretation and construction.[57] Other than these mentioned principles, there is the method of *qiyās* to establish an opinion and a legal rule.[58] In general, it is extraction of legal rules by analogy. This is a main part of *ijtihād*, practised by the four Sunnī *madhhabs* and therefore a part of *fiqh*.[59] *Qiyās* is the fourth source of Islamic Law.[60] The function is to expand legal rules of the revealed texts, in cases which are not mentioned.[61] This could be cases about modern legal issues or problems, which are too specific to be mentioned. *Qiyās* is rooted in the *Qur'an*, which justifies the use and makes it acceptable.[62] The main idea of *qiyās* is to derive the ratio legis from a verse of the *Qur'an* or a *hadīth*.[63] The extracted ratio legis is called *'illa*.[64] This *'illa* is transferable to a new problematic case when they both share the same operative clause.[65] By means of transfer of the general legal idea behind the old rule, new cases are solvable. For example, if a question comes up about what sentence a guardian of an orphan has to expect, when he burns the personal property of the orphan.[66] The *Qur'an* says about this: "Indeed, those who devour the property of orphans unjustly are only

---

56 N J Coulson, *loc. cit.*, p.78
57 N J Coulson, *loc. cit.*, p.78
58 N J Coulson, *loc. cit.*, p.59
59 K Vikor, *loc. cit.*, p.31
60 N J Coulson, *loc. cit.*, p.59
61 K Vikor, *loc. cit.*, p.53
62 K Vikor, *loc. cit.*, p.54-5
63 K A El Fadl, *loc. cit.*, p.36
64 K Vikor, *loc. cit.*, p.58
65 K A El Fadl, *loc. cit.*, p.36
66 Sheikh W b. I al-`Ujajî, *'Qiyas in Islamic Law – A Brief Introduction'* (2007) Pt. A – No. 1, <http://en.islamtoday.net/artshow-385-3387.htm> accessed 05th November 2014

consuming into their bellies fire. And they will be burned in a Blaze." [4:10]. The literal text only includes the expenditure of the orphans property for the guardian himself. Consequently, burning the wealth is not occupied by the rule and so the guardian does not have to expect any punishment according to this rule. Obviously, this result is not satisfying. Therefore legal scholars deduce the *'illa* behind the qur'anic verse. In this example, the *'illa* is to protect orphans wealth from being lost beyond recall and to punish guardians, if they are responsible.[67] In the example, the guardian burns the orphans personal property. Consequently, it is lost and the orphan can not profit from it. To draw a conclusion from this, the *'illa* is the same in both cases and so the punishment is transferable from the qur'anic verse to the new case.[68] The guardian has to expect the same sentence. A general legal rule is established by use of analogy on the specific rule. Central requirement is the same *'illa* in both cases.

To summarise derivation of Islamic Law, we have to focus on the four sources. These are the *Qur'an* as the first and the *Sunnah* as the second source. Both texts are revealed by God. From this follows that there can not be any discussions about the legal rules directly extracted from them, because God can not fail. Arguable is only the human formation of opinions through *fiqh* as Islamic jurisprudence, because humans can fail in interpreting the words of God. *Fiqh* includes, beside other techniques, the third source *ijmā'* and the fourth source *qiyās*. The system of the four sources is also expressible in a three level system. The first level includes the *Qur'an* and the *Sunnah*.[69] The second level is work on the texts of the first level. After understanding this texts,

---
67 Sheikh W b. I al-`Ujajî, *loc. Cit.*, Pt. A – No. 1
68 Sheikh W b. I al-`Ujajî, *loc. Cit.*, Pt. A – No. 1
69 K Vikor, *loc. cit.*, p.31

lawyers deduce legal rules from them, considering God's will.[70] This interpretation of the *Qur'an* and the *Sunnah* with the result to develop new legal rules is called *ijtihād*,[71] practised by the *madhhabs*.[72] One of the most important methods to do this is *qiyās*. This results in many different contradictory interpretations of the texts, due to the number of lawyers and the influence of their *madhhab*. Elimination of interpretations take place at the third level, executed by legal scholars of the *madhhabs*.[73] Part of this third level is the source of *ijmā'*. To reach a conclusion, Islamic Law in general comes from the unification of the four sources. An applicable legal rule can be established through the three levels starting at the first moving to the third level.[74]

---

70 K Vikor, *loc. cit.*, p.31
71 K Vikor, *loc. cit.*, p.352
72 K Vikor, *loc. cit.*, p.32
73 K Vikor, *loc. cit.*, p.32
74 K Vikor, *loc. cit.*, p.32

Bibliography

Al-`Ujajî Sheikh Walîd b. Ibrâhîm , *Qiyas in Islamic Law – A Brief Introduction* (islamtoday.net, 2007), <http://en.islamtoday.net/artshow-385-3387.htm> accessed 5th November 2014

Calder N, Kéchichian J A, Ziadeh F J, Sachedina A, Hendrickson J, Mayer A E, Rabb I A, 'Law.' in *The Oxford Encyclopedia of the Islamic World. Oxford Islamic Studies Online*, <http://www.oxfordislamicstudies.com/article/opr/t236/e0473> accessed 5th November 2014

Coulson N J, *A History of Islamic Law* (Edinburgh: Edinburgh University Press, 1964)

El Fadl K A, *Speaking in God's Name: Islamic Law, Authority, and Women* (Oxford: Oneworld Publications, 2001)

Vikor K, *Between God and the Sultan: A History of Islamic Law* (London: C. Hurst & Co. LTD., 2005)

YOUR KNOWLEDGE HAS VALUE

- We will publish your bachelor's and master's thesis, essays and papers

- Your own eBook and book - sold worldwide in all relevant shops

- Earn money with each sale

Upload your text at www.GRIN.com
and publish for free